THE GIFT
OF SOBRIETY

◆

D1554673

THE GIFT
OF SOBRIETY

◆

112 REASONS NOT
TO DRINK TODAY

New World Library
San Rafael, California

© 1993 New World Library

Published by New World Library
58 Paul Drive
San Rafael, CA 94903

Cover Design: John A. Helgeson
Cover Photo: Dean Campbell
Text Design & Typography: Becky Benenate

Printed in the U.S.A. on acid-free paper
ISBN 1-880032-24-4
10 9 8 7 6 5 4 3 2

◆

"The past is gone; the future is but a dream. We have only today, my friends, which is a gift from God — that's why we call it the *present*."

— Anonymous

CONTENTS

♦

112 Reasons Not to Drink Today

INTRODUCTION

◆

This little book is the result of the contributions of a number of former drinkers and recovering alcoholics. Among us, we represent a great many years of both problem drinking and successful recovery.

For all of us, sobriety is the greatest gift we have received. There are at least 112 reasons for this, and we're certain every ex-drinker can add more reasons of their own.

One of the greatest fears many of us have is that, despite all the very good reasons we have for staying clean and sober, we will in an impulsive moment forget everything and have that first drink or that first drug.

Some of us have found it useful to carry a list of reasons not to drink around with us; we offer our reasons to you in this little book. Some may be applicable to you, some may not.

There is extra paper in the back to add your own reasons not to have a drink today. Your own reasons, in your own words, are the best reasons of all.

It is our heartfelt wish that this little book may help you become healthy, happy, and fulfilled in life. And, even more importantly, may it help you to stay clean and sober.

◆

"I have come to believe that the gift of sobriety is what gives value and dignity to my life. It is this that I have to share, and it grows as it is shared."

— Anonymous
Came to Believe

THE GIFT
OF SOBRIETY

◆

I

PERSONAL REASONS

NOT TO DRINK TODAY

♦

♦ 1 ♦

Each day that I am sober is a gift.

♦ 2 ♦

I've realized that I'm unable to control my drinking — therefore, I won't even have one.

♦ 3 ♦

Alcohol is a sedative; it depletes my energy and robs me of real joy, creativity, and fulfillment.

♦ 4 ♦

I have the choice of two paths before me — at every moment. One ascends to happiness, serenity, power, success, making a positive contribution to humanity. One descends to drunkenness, misery, loneliness, poverty, ugliness, failure, disease, and jail. To choose the first path, I must be clean and sober. The second path requires just one drink....

♦ 5 ♦

Everything changes, everything passes. Any impulse I have to drink, as well as any boredom, irritation, or cynicism I have, will soon pass.

♦ 6 ♦

Alcohol has become my enemy, not my friend.

♦ 7 ♦

I know my drinking habits all too well:
If I have one drink, I'll want one more; if I
have one more, I'll want another, then
another, then another.... "One drink is too
many; 1,000 drinks are not enough."

♦ 8 ♦

My attempts to control my drinking
were but half measures, and they didn't
work. "Half measures availed us noth-
ing."

— *Alcoholics Anonymous*, p. 59

♦ 9 ♦

I had reached the point where I was
preoccupied with alcohol; I spent far too
much of my precious time drinking. My
life is no longer preoccupied with drinking;

I now have so much more time to spend on worthwhile and enjoyable things.

◆ 10 ◆

My sobriety is the single most important thing in my life — without it, all is lost.

◆ 11 ◆

I surrender to the fact that I cannot drink like other people, and this surrender is a positive and creative force in my life.

◆ 12 ◆

As soon as I have had one drink, I put far too much time and energy into getting and having my next drink. I like the freedom of having the whole rest of the day or night in front of me, without having to waste any time or energy drinking.

♦ 13 ♦

I no longer live my life in an alcohol-induced fog.

♦ 14 ♦

Drinking alcohol reactivates the phenomenon of craving for more alcohol. I don't want to live my life under the shadow of a craving for alcohol.

♦ 15 ♦

When I was drinking, there were far too many days and nights when I was wiped out early in the afternoon or evening. Without drinking, I'm clearheaded and energetic late into the evening — and can get up early, feeling good.

♦ 16 ♦

"When I was finally guided into our

Fellowship, I thought it would be a dull routine at best, free from the tyranny of booze but lived under a constant sky of deadly grey. The surprise I got at finding the little delights of sheer living again was one of the treasures AA brought to me."

— *Best of the Grapevine II*, p. 77

♦ 17 ♦

Our society is cracking down on excessive use of alcohol; there are now mandatory jail sentences for driving under the influence.

♦ 18 ♦

"Staying sober opens up the way to life and happiness."

— *Living Sober*, p. 13

♦ 19 ♦

"God grant me the serenity to accept the things I cannot change, the courage to change the things I can, and the wisdom to know the difference." I cannot change the fact that I am addicted to alcohol, but I can change my living habits — and refuse to take a drink today.

♦ 20 ♦

I have been sober now for x number of days, weeks, months, or years. I want to maintain and enjoy my continuous sobriety.

♦ 21 ♦

I am a master of massive denial. Staying sober leads me, day by day, to a positive form of mastery — a mastery of my habits, a mastery of my life.

♦ 22 ♦

I have seen from the painful experiences of others (or have known from my own painful experience) that a relapse would only lead to a powerfully negative experience that I don't need in my life.

♦ 23 ♦

Living sober is a joyous experience.

♦ 24 ♦

I simply have to keep away from the first dose of a drug that I have become addicted to: alcohol. I pray and pledge that I will not drink for this one day, today. My sobriety today brings great rewards into my life.

♦ 25 ♦

As it says in the Bible, alcohol "bites

like a snake and stings like a viper."

— *Proverbs 23, vs. 21*

♦ 26 ♦

In this moment, I have the gift of sobriety. I don't want to throw this gift away, for it is the most precious possession I have.

♦ 27 ♦

You can change a cucumber into a pickle, but you can't change a pickle back into a cucumber. I've been "pickled" enough by alcohol — I've been drunk enough times to know I can't revert back to a controlled social drinker.

♦ 28 ♦

Just for today, I will act like someone I admire — someone who is clean and sober.

♦ 29 ♦

If I relapsed, I'd feel truly lousy. The guilt, shame, and sadness would be far worse than any momentary high or oblivion I might experience from drinking.

♦ 30 ♦

For every adversity in my life, there is an equal or greater benefit. "God brings difficulties into our lives to make us better, not bitter."

> — Dan Reeves, former head
> coach of the Denver Broncos

♦ 31 ♦

I have a contribution to make, in my own personal way, by my own example, to the great recovery movement that is spreading throughout the world.

♦ 32 ♦

As long as I abstain from drinking, infinite possibilities and opportunities stretch before me. When drinking, my possibilities are extremely limited.

♦ 33 ♦

Drinking is not an option for me — my past experience has proven this conclusively.

♦ 34 ♦

Drinking isn't fun anymore.

♦ 35 ♦

"Alcoholics usually have no idea why they take the first drink... but the first drink sets the terrible cycle in motion."

— *Twenty-four Hours*, Aug. 11

◆ 36 ◆

"I call drugs and alcohol the great tricksters because they hide their true faces from our view. They begin by enhancing the ordinary, but end in their own darkness."

— *Letters to My Son*, p. 68

◆ 37 ◆

"Drinking is a devil's bargain. You get something extra in the present, but you pay for it in the future. And you never know the real price until it is due."

— *Letters to My Son*, p. 70

◆ 38 ◆

My sobriety is the foundation upon which I am building the good life.

◆

II

SOCIAL REASONS

NOT TO DRINK TODAY

♦

♦ 39 ♦

I've reached the point where sobriety is definitely a better high than alcohol-induced lethargy.

♦ 40 ♦

Drinking destroys my self-esteem, which affects my personal relationships with others.

♦ 41 ♦

Sobriety is so enjoyable — there is no

shame, no fear of drunk driving or other drunken acts.

♦ 42 ♦

I have so much more energy in the evenings — to read, to enjoy my friends and my family.

♦ 43 ♦

I have proven to myself that I cannot drink like a "normal" person, so I have forfeited the privilege of drinking alcohol.

♦ 44 ♦

Alcohol is so filling that it ruins a good meal. In sobriety, I can truly enjoy a good meal again, and a great many other simple pleasures as well.

◆ 45 ◆

We all do what we think is "cool." In the '60s and '70s, substance abuse was cool. In the '90s, it isn't. Sobriety is cool.

◆ 46 ◆

"While you were drinking, you were withdrawing from life little by little. Now you are getting back into the social life of this world."

— *Alcoholics Anonymous*, p. 102

◆ 47 ◆

I crossed the line from enjoyable social drinking into addictive, nightly craving. I can't drink like most people — I can't ever get back to enjoyable social drinking, without wanting another, and another, and then suffering the consequences of excessive alcohol abuse.

♦ 48 ♦

So many lost evenings... and lost weekends. I don't ever want to experience those losses in my life again.

♦ 49 ♦

"We have found we can enjoy, sober, every good thing we enjoyed while drinking — and many, many more."

— *Living Sober*, p. 42

♦ 50 ♦

If I don't take that first drink, I won't get drunk, I won't get out of control and I won't get into trouble.

♦ 51 ♦

The drunken party's over.... The clean and sober party has just begun.

♦ 52 ♦

"Living sober turns out to be not at all grim, boring, and uncomfortable, as we had feared, but rather something we begin to enjoy and find much more exciting than our drinking days."

— *Living Sober*, Introduction

♦ 53 ♦

If I drink today, there will be serious repercussions, which would most likely include a great many things I can foresee and a great many things I cannot foresee.

♦ 54 ♦

It feels so fine to be bright and alert at

a party (or any social function) late in the evening.

♦ 55 ♦

I've said and done things while drinking that I have regretted later.

♦ 56 ♦

I am free to drive anywhere, any hour, without restriction or paranoia.

♦

III

FAMILY REASONS

NOT TO DRINK TODAY

♦

♦ 57 ♦

I want to be sober for my family. My parents (or my children or significant other or close friends) are proud of me for not drinking.

♦ 58 ♦

A number of friends and relatives I love would be hurt and deeply disappointed if I take that first drink.

♦ 59 ♦

I can share so many more precious moments with others when I am sober. When drinking, I cannot relate to others as intimately and effectively.

♦ 60 ♦

A drink will reactivate my chemical dependency, which has been defined by therapists at some treatment centers as "gradual deterioration of all areas of a person's personality and family."

♦ 61 ♦

I am fully present for my family — a true gift of sobriety.

♦ 62 ♦

At this point in my life, after what I've been through, even one little drink will only make things worse for everyone.

◆ 63 ◆

Only by staying sober can I be the family person I want to be.

◆ 64 ◆

My actions have repercussions that affect so many people. If I remain sober, the repercussions of my actions are wonderfully positive; if I drink they are horrendously negative.

◆ 65 ◆

I need to remember the words of the concerned, loving people in my life when I was drinking — words that were difficult for them to say: "You are an alcoholic." "You don't know when to quit." "Do you want to be drunk 75 percent of the time?"

"Do you want to have alcoholic children?" They were said out of love and concern.

◆ 66 ◆

So many people, family members and others, are delighted and encouraged by my sobriety.

◆ 67 ◆

When I was drinking, all of those close to me were forced to "ignore the elephant in the living room." I had a major problem in my life that I couldn't or wouldn't confront, and a great many others suffered because of it.

◆

IV

FINANCIAL AND PROFESSIONAL REASONS NOT TO DRINK TODAY

♦

♦ 68 ♦

A new life of limitless possibilities and opportunities is before me, if I refrain from taking that first drink.

♦ 69 ♦

I know my beliefs are powerful and self-reinforcing, so I have developed this simple belief: If I don't drink, my life will work a lot better.

♦ 70 ♦

My personal and financial goals will not be met if I drink.

♦ 71 ♦

Drinking is expensive.

♦ 72 ♦

Alcohol depreciates my self-worth, which affects my value to others and my ability to create the life I want financially.

♦ 73 ♦

If I don't take a drink today, I've done the perfect thing.... I'm successful, regardless of any other circumstances in my life today.

♦ 74 ♦

Drinking undermines my chances for success. My money evaporates, and my

dependability and credibility at work are
severely damaged.

♦ 75 ♦

In my drinking days, I could feel my
power and effectiveness declining as a
businessperson, worker, speaker, and
thinker.

♦ 76 ♦

When I don't drink, my star rises.
When I drink, my star fades.

♦ 77 ♦

I feel better, stronger, more confident
in my working relationships when not
drinking.

♦ 78 ♦

"The important point is that sobriety
has to have first priority, for without it no

other significant life improvements are
possible."

— *Under the Influence,* p. 146

♦ 79 ♦

By not drinking, I have the freedom to
pursue my dreams, without limitation. As
a speaker in a meeting said, "It'll be
beyond your wildest dreams."

♦ 80 ♦

So many famous artists, writers, and
business leaders have succeeded for many
years by staying sober; so many of them
have rapidly gone down hill when drinking. I want to follow the example of the
successful, sober ones.

♦ 81 ♦

I am an effective, powerful worker and

leader when I am clean and sober. This is something to be justifiably proud of.

♦ 82 ♦

I am not proud of myself or of my accomplishments when drinking.

♦ 83 ♦

I remember thinking in my drinking era that those who didn't drink had an advantage over me in their careers. I now have the power of my sobriety working for me.

♦ 84 ♦

I felt separate from others and isolated when entering my place of work after drinking. When sober, I am open and free, able to joke and laugh with others — and work with others to the best of my capability.

◆ 85 ◆

My drinking has an insidious, pervasive effect on those around me. It definitely hurts the performance of my co-workers, and the bottom line of the business suffers.

◆

V

HEALTH REASONS
NOT TO DRINK TODAY

♦

♦ 86 ♦

Remember: Alcoholism is an incurable, progressive, fatal disease.

♦ 87 ♦

I've already drank and used enough for one lifetime.

♦ 88 ♦

I'm in recovery, which has been defined as "gradual restoration to good health of body, mind, and spirit."

♦ 89 ♦

In my sobriety, the sparkle has come back into my eyes.

♦ 90 ♦

I love waking in the morning, refreshed after a good night's sleep, healthy, remembering with a clear head the previous evening's activities.

♦ 91 ♦

I don't eat properly when drinking.

♦ 92 ♦

"Why does he continue to drink when drinking is slowly but surely destroying him?"

— *Under the Influence*, p. 94

♦ 93 ♦

"Virtually all the effective (treatment) programs have in common the understanding that alcoholism is a disease that can be arrested but not cured and that the cornerstone of full recovery must be continuous total abstinence from alcohol and substitute drugs."

— *Under the Influence*, p. 144

♦ 94 ♦

No more hangovers! I used to wake up feeling poisoned in the mornings.

♦ 95 ♦

Quitting drinking has improved my digestion and regularity.

♦ 96 ♦

I have a great reason not to drink whenever I recall the faces of my ex-drinking buddies — red, flushed, with glazed eyes, old before their time. My face when drinking was red and bloated, and blood vessels had broken out on my nose and cheeks. An alcoholic face is not a pretty thing.

♦ 97 ♦

Drinking adversely affects testosterone levels and sperm count in men, and sexual performance in general. Sober sex is the greatest! Women are even more susceptible to the harmful effects of alcohol than men are; and drinking during pregnancy is, of course, extremely harmful to the unborn baby.

◆ 98 ◆

I am at an age where my body can deteriorate quickly, if I continue to drink — or stay strong and healthy, if I continue to abstain from drinking.

◆ 99 ◆

After my first three weeks of sobriety, I looked five years younger. My face was no longer red and bloated, and I was slimmer and healthier looking.

◆ 100 ◆

"Real drinkers have willpower. The trick we learned was to put that will to work for our health, and to make ourselves explore recovery ideas at great depth, even though it sometimes might have seemed like drudgery."

— *Living Sober*, p. 85

♦ 101 ♦

Alcohol abuse can worsen the diseases associated with aging, particularly heart disease and hypertension.

♦ 102 ♦

Alcohol abuse poisons your lungs and liver, inflames your pancreas, and lowers your resistance to disease by decreasing your white and red blood cell production.

♦ 103 ♦

Alcohol abuse causes loss of memory and concentration, kills brain cells, and can lead to long-term brain damage.

♦

VI

SPIRITUAL REASONS

NOT TO DRINK TODAY

♦

♦ 104 ♦

Somehow, in an almost mystical way, I have discovered that as I continue not to drink, there is far more to live for in my life. Every moment is filled with wonder; just being alive is a magical experience.

♦ 105 ♦

Remember the serenity prayer: the promise of the prayer is that, without drinking, I can truly achieve serenity.

♦ 106 ♦

If I drink, I'll miss the cumulative magic that happens at AA meetings. "If alcoholics persevere, and continue to attend the meetings, they find a mystic magic there, an indefinable spiritual quality that permeates them and helps them not to drink and to want to become completely well."

— *Best of the Grapevine II*, p. 52

♦ 107 ♦

My higher power wants me to be happy, joyous, and free.

♦ 108 ♦

My higher power does not want me to drink. "Follow the dictates of a higher power and you will presently live in a new and wonderful world, no matter what your present circumstances."

— *Alcoholics Anonymous*, p. 100

◆ 109 ◆

I want to work the twelve steps all my life, and help others to work them. I know that the result is a true connection with a higher power, and a life well lived.

◆ 110 ◆

I lose my connection with a Higher Power when drinking.

◆ 111 ◆

The first day of my sobriety was _____. This date is meaningful to me, more meaningful in many ways than the day I was born. It is the day in which I started a new life, one filled with hope, love, and dreams. I do not

want to drink today, because I want to
keep the date of my sobriety intact, and I
want to continue the spiritual awakening
that is miraculously unfolding in my life.

◆ 112 ◆

I have been promised: I will have a
spiritual awakening, as long as I do not
drink today.

◆

◆

"Is sobriety all that we are to expect of a spiritual awakening? No, sobriety is only a bare beginning; it is only the first gift of the first awakening.

"If more gifts are to be received, our awakening has to go on. As it does go on, we find that bit by bit we can discard the old life — the one that did not work — for a new life that can and does work under any conditions whatever."

— Bill W.
A.A. Grapevine, Dec., 1957

MORE REASONS NOT TO DRINK TODAY:

MORE REASONS NOT TO DRINK TODAY:

_____

_____

_____

_____

_____

_____

_____

_____

_____

_____

_____

_____

_____

_____

_____

_____

MORE REASONS NOT TO DRINK TODAY:

_____

_____

_____

_____

_____

_____

_____

_____

_____

_____

_____

_____

_____

_____

_____

_____

_____

MORE REASONS NOT TO DRINK TODAY:

MORE REASONS NOT TO DRINK TODAY:

_____

_____

_____

_____

_____

_____

_____

_____

_____

_____

_____

_____

_____

_____

_____

_____

MORE REASONS NOT TO DRINK TODAY:

MORE REASONS NOT TO DRINK TODAY:

New World Library is dedicated to publishing books and cassettes that help improve the quality of our lives. If you enjoyed *The Gift of Sobriety*, we highly recommend the following books from New World Library:

Reflections in the Light by Shakti Gawain. A pocket-sized collection of inspiring thoughts and affirmations from the author's classic books, designed to be read every day of any calendar year. (Paperback, $9.95)

Letters to My Son — Reflections on Becoming a Man by Kent Nerburn. This highly acclaimed book is filled with brilliant, heartfelt advice on being male, love and sex, drugs and alcohol, education, work, money, spirituality and other important subjects. (Hardcover, $14.95)

As You Think by James Allen. This

classic has inspired readers for nearly a century. The key to our happiness and personal power is in our minds, and we can learn how to unlock the door to our success, however we may define it. (Paperback, $6.95; Hardcover Gift Edition $9.95)

The Perfect Life by Marc Allen. This powerful book shows you step by step how to clearly define what you want in life, and how to map a course that moves you toward the realization of your dreams. (Paperback, $9.95)

The Gift of Sobriety is also available in a smaller pocket edition for $2.95.

The cover photo, entitled **"First Light,"** by nature photographer Dean Campbell, is available as a matted print in several sizes. (8x10," $75; 11x14," $100; 16x20," $125)

For a complete catalog of our fine
books and cassettes, contact:

New World Library
58 Paul Drive
San Rafael, CA 94903

Phone: (415) 472-2100
FAX: (415) 472-6131

Or call toll-free:
(800) 227-3900
In California: (800) 632-2122